Whirling Winds

A Collection of Poems

Whirling Winds

India | USA | UK

Made with ❤ on the BookLeaf Publishing Platform
www.bookleafpub.in
www.bookleafpub.com

Dedication

To my mother, Anusha, who made me who I am today.

Acknowledgement

First, a huge thank you to my mother for always believing in me and for guiding me in all that I do. Without her support, this book would not have been possible. Next, I thank Priya Aunty for teaching me new words and helping me improve my writing skills. I also thank Sarayu Aunty for appreciating and encouraging me every time she reads my poems. Finally, I would like to thank Book Leaf Publishing and all its team members who worked hard to bring this book to life and for giving me a platform to share my poems.

Preface

Hello everyone!

I am Vidyut, and I am eight years old. I am excited to share that this is my very first published book. I wrote it because I wanted to share all of my ideas with all of you.
Writing makes me feel both confident and excited, and I love crafting poems or stories whenever I have some free time.

Since I was a baby, my mother has read many stories to me and regularly taken my younger brother and me to the library. I have always enjoyed reading both fiction and encyclopaedias equally. The more I started to read, the more inspired I became to write my own poems.

Thank you so much for reading my poems. I hope they brighten your day and make you feel happy!

1. BLACK AND WHITE

Black and white, the opposites.
Black is dark and white is light.
Black is the night sky upon which are the white twinkling stars.
Black is the deep, damp forest through which the clean white river flows.
Black is the umbrella that protects us from the white pitter-patter raindrops.
Black is dark chocolate that tops a cone of white vanilla ice cream.
Black is the crow, which is friendly with the white dove.
Black is the smoke from the white burning fire.
Black is the hair that changes to white when we grow old.

Both black and white are the eyes that see all the colours around us!

2. INDEPENDENCE DAY AT SCHOOL

The Independence Day of victorious India
Falls on August fifteenth.
We salute our National Flag
Which is orange, blue, white and green.

We hoist our National Flag
In our sandy and rocky school grounds.
And when we hear our national anthem
In our hearts, freedom is found.

All the schoolchildren must stand straight
When the National Anthem is being played,
We should sing along with love and pride
With our hearts as bright as light.

3. FIVE ELEMENTS

Air is something we cannot see but can feel,
It helps us breathe, which is a great big deal!

Water we can drink, swim in and play,
It is so special, and it never makes us feel grey.

Fire is very hot, flaming and ever-burning,
Once touched, into a scar our skin will be
turning.

Space is everywhere, from the vast galaxies to our
homes and cities,
With no walls or forts around it, space extends for
Infinity.

Earth holds life and land and gives us food,
We receive strength and steadiness from it,
making us ready for a day that's good.

These are the five elements that make our life a
Celebration!

4. DUCKS

A LIMERICK

Ducks are the funniest birds in the world,
We can roast them and eat them with curd.
But with some luck of the duck
It can escape from being stuck!
And a 'quack quack'" can be heard.

5. THE TOWN OF FRYPETTAI

Frypettai is a miniature town
Located to the south, oh so down!
It is a town where no one frowns
And famous for its paintings, bags and gowns.

It also publishes a large number of books
Everyone rocks and rolls, but not with crooks.
They drop the crooks with their fishing rod hooks,
Into the Bay of Fryers, which is a small, narrow
brook.

6. MOVEMENT OF ANIMALS

Once lived a Whale
Who was an expert in swimming,
He swam and swam until he got winning.

Once lived a Snake
Who was skilled in slithering,
He slithered and slithered until he got winning.

Once lived a Kangaroo
Who was the master of hopping,
He hopped and hopped until he got winning.

Once lived a Cat
Who was experienced in trotting,
He trotted and trotted until he got winning.

Once lived a Penguin
Who was good at waddling,
He waddled and waddled until he got winning.

Once lived a Tiger
Who was talented at leaping,
He leaped and leaped until he got winning.

Once lived an Eagle
Who was excellent at soaring,
He soared and soared until he got winning.

Once lived a human
Who always killed them all,
He killed and killed until he got losing.

7. FRIENDS AND FOES

A DIAMANTE POEM

Friends
Witty, loyal
Playing, caring, sharing
Buddy, teammate, *enemy, nemesis*
Hitting, pushing, punching
Unwelcoming, angry
Foe

8. RACING CARS

One Ferrari zooming on the road
Two Lamborghinis fixing their spoilers
Three Nissans stopping at traffic signals
Four Hyundais standing in a row
Five Hondas parked outside a café
Six Bentleys climbing over the flyovers
Seven Benzes getting ready for a race
Eight Jeeps with engines roaring
Nine Audis speeding across the snow
Ten Maseratis bolting away like lightning.

9. NATURAL

11. TRIP TO THE MOVIES

Watching the gigantic Dinosaurs on a massive
screen,,
Was my first ever royal movie experience, like a
dream.
A t-rex lifting a jeep and throwing it aside
with a few scared people screaming and sitting
inside.
Whether on a rainy day or a stormy night
The hero's team bravely fought with all their
might.

And then was the movie Frozen coming up next
in line,
Everything was good and it was just fine.
There was Elsa and Anna walking through
hailstorms, blizzards and snow,
As they helped each other, their love started to
grow.
Olaf, Sven and Marshmallow,
Accompanied the siblings along with Kristoff the
handsome fellow.

Next was the Panda movie, which was really funny
and cool
And one of the evil characters was such a big fool.
The sorceress shape-shifted into Tai Lung,
LordShen and General Kai,
But Po just crushed her superpowers and made
her cry.
The Panda's fathers were kind and friendly to him
always,
They never doubted his abilities or hurt him, No
way!

And this is how my movie-going experiences went
by!

14. ODE TO THE PYRAMIDS

Oh, the Pyramids of Giza!
You're as old as time.
Standing next to you in the scorching desert heat,
Makes me feel sweaty, but still my heart chimes.

Oh, the Pyramids of Giza!
You're as tall as the mighty K2 mountains.
You always supported the ancient Egyptians,
And looking at you makes me jump with

16. AIRPLANES

Airplanes fly high, very high,
they love to fly on long journeys,
in the blue, blue sky,
with clear air and white clouds.

Don't be scared when the plane shakes,
when it gets all rainy and wet.
And you all have a safe trip,
as you soar into the sky.

17. OCEAN WATERS

Oceans are white, oceans are transparent,
Oceans are salty, oceans are deep.
Oceans are fun to swim and play,
Oceans are dangerous and violent that make us
weep.

Oceans help to start the water cycle,
Oceans form waves near the beach, where I love
to soak my feet.
Oceans also cause tsunamis and floods,
Oceans are home to aquatic animals that you can
meet.

18. SUMMER AND WINTER

A DIAMANTE POEM

Summer
Hot, bright
Melting, scorching, relaxing
Beach, ice cream, *snowman, blizzard*
Freezing, snowing, shivering
Cold, gloomy
Winter

19. THIS LITTLE HAND

This little hand planted a tiny seed,
This little hand watered the precious seed,
This little hand put the mud pot under the yellow
sun,
This little hand happily cared for the baby plant,
This little hand carefully plucked the weeds,
This little hand nurtured the plant as if it were his
own.
And this big hand enjoyed the fruits, flowers and
shade from the gigantic tree.

20. FUNNY MONKEYS

A LIMERICK

Monkeys chant oo-oo ah-ah!
They are always friends with Cinderella.
They all get naughty and start scratching,
When they slide on the sand under the hot sun
dancing.
And so, they won't be stolen like the Dalmatians
by Cruella.

21. BEAUTY

Beautiful are the eyes of my mother that look like
diamonds,
Beauty is the kajal lined on my mother's sparkly
eyes.

Beautiful is the sea, which I love to stare at night
time,
Beauty is the rainbow that comes after a storm in
the evening.

Beautiful are the luxury cars that I really want to
drive one day,
Beauty is the airport lights that shine when the
plane lands.

Beautiful is my brick house, which was newly
painted this summer,
Beauty is the wooden table around which my
family sits and eats every day.

Beautiful are the high towers that soar towards
the blue skies
Beauty is the bridge that connects them for
people to walk between the two buildings

Beauty is found everywhere, around me and you,
And that's how I want it to be, always and forever.

9 789363 306530